THE STRATEGIC SLIDE

A Trader's Guide to Mastering Profits with a Simple and Proven Averaging Down Strategy

PAMELA S BATOON

Book Design by HMDpublishing

DEDICATION

This book is dedicated to all of the ambitious souls who dare to navigate the financial markets. It is for both the novice and seasoned trader either taking their first steps into this dynamic trading world and are looking for guidance or have already forged paths and are looking for a fresh perspective and strategy to enhance trading prowess.

My goal is that the pages within serve as a compass, leading you through a dynamic yet lower risk trading strategy that will have you earning profits in no time.

It is not a get-rich scheme, rather, it is a meticulously thought-out trading plan that emphasizes long-term growth and sustainability. By following the strategy outlined in these pages, you'll be equipped with the knowledge and tools to make informed decisions and manage risk effectively. Remember, successful trading requires discipline, patience and continuous learning. This guide aims to provide you with the essential foundation for a prosperous trading journey.

CONTENTS

INTRODUCTION

Buy low, sell high. Buy the gap. Sell the gap. Short the news. Trade the Fibonacci retracement. Buy and hold forever. Diversify. Never put all of your eggs in one basket. I'm a day trader. No wait, I'm a swing trader. Well, now the stock has dropped even more so I'll switch to a long-term investor. Yeah, that'll do it.

In the dynamic world of financial markets, where fortunes are made and lost in the blink of an eye, experience is the truest compass. For over twenty-five years, I have navigated the intricate labyrinth of trading and investing, weathering market storms and riding waves of prosperity.

Through booms and busts, I have deployed a number of trading strategies – some with great success and others, not so much. And while I've seen strategies come and go like the seasons, there exists a singular approach that has remained steadfast.

In these pages, I invite you to embark on a journey of discovery, one that will have you adding a new, consistently profitable trading strategy to your portfolio. Whether you are a seasoned trader seeking fresh perspectives or a novice investor eager to get started, this book offers insights into a strategy that requires few analytics and reduced risk.

This book is not a compendium of various techniques or a summary dissertation of fleeting trends. Instead, it is a deep dive into the heart of a single, meticulously crafted methodology. Together, we will dissect the approach by understanding the underlying principles and unravel the intricacies that make it a formidable tool in the hands of a discerning trader.

Throughout these pages, you will discover the nuts and bolts of this strategy including how to approach entry and exit points that reduces risk and maximizes profit potential based on actual trades. We will also delve into the proper mindset as well as cover the two simple analytical tools used for analysis.

It is my hope that within these pages you will find the building blocks to develop and build upon a deep understanding of a single, potent strategy.

Now dear reader, let us begin.

CHAPTER 1

INTRODUCING: THE STRATEGIC SLIDE

Entering the world of trading is one of the most profound, exhilarating journeys one could embark upon. In no other profession, or hobby, will you even come close to the extreme up and down swings of an active day. The winnings can be swift and enormous. The losses, if you are careless, can take you out of the trading game forever. And with so many technical strategies requiring expertise in charting and indicator analysis, it's no wonder that most new traders unwillingly gift their hard-earned money away to the trader on the other side.

The good news is, you can absolutely and consistently make profits with one simple trading strategy. I call it: 'The Strategic Slide'.

Strategic slide is very similar to the concept of averaging down, referring to the strategy in which an investor or trader buys more of a particular asset at a lower price than their initial purchase price with the aim of reducing the average cost per unit of the asset. This is done when the price of the asset has decreased after the initial purchase. What sets the Strategic Slide strategy apart is that the criteria around stock selection and price entry points provides for an overall lower risk-to-reward ratio.

I use this technique over and over using this specific criteria and often profit trading the same stock multiple times with this strategy. And the best part is, you only need a few simple indicators for an insightful analysis. I've done it over and over resulting in steady profits and I am excited to share this simple strategy with you. But before we get into the nuts and bolts of this strategy, it's important to first approach trading with the right mind set.

CHAPTER 2

DEVELOPING THE TRADER'S MIND

The desire for the "big" score is one of the most recognizable traits of a novice trader. Though a novice may occasionally get lucky and hit pay dirt with a home run, this will never sustain the novice over the long term.

The true professional is after the smaller yet consistent, more predictable gains. They have a game plan of what they plan to buy, at what price they will enter the stock, at what price they will exit the stock for profits and most importantly, at what price they will exit the stock in the event the stock moves against them.

This last component is what gets novice traders all the time. They have great intentions to be disciplined about selling at a specific price point but when a price goes against them, the second-guessing starts blowing up their brains. "Well, let me look at this chart again. Maybe I'm keeping my stop-loss too tight. Yeah, I see a little more wiggle room. Wait, what? What the…well, dang-it all. Now I'm down way too much so I HAVE to hold. Hmmm…I wonder if I should buy more? Folks on social media site Reddit seem to think this is going to go back up. But if I look at this subscription service I recently joined, it looks like there are more puts than calls. Maybe if I just close my eyes for 5 minutes and open them back up the stock will be back to where I should have sold in the first place. But if it gets there, then that means it's going up, so, I should hold on for more upward movement…right? HELP!"

Does that sound like anyone you know? Trust me. Been there, done that.

And it's not just the situation of bailing on the original plan and being either stuck in a position or taking a deeper loss when I couldn't take-it-anymore. How about the many times I did stick to my stop-loss strategy only to watch the stock climb right back up? Do you really think I congratulated myself for sticking with my strategy versus admonishing the fact I had just lost out on a higher gain? Did I congratulate myself for having more wins than losses? Nope. Losing sucks. Period.

The secret to consistent profits is approaching trading with the purpose to learn to trade well. If you trade well, the profits will take care of itself.

CHAPTER 3

LEARNING TO TRADE TO TRADE WELL (NOT TO MAKE MONEY)

One of the biggest mistakes a new trader can make is the continual calculation of profits in their head while in the trade. Nothing blows your concentration and clouds your judgment more than keeping this mental tab running in your head counting up the gained or lost dollars with each tick price. Instead of sticking to your originally well thought-out plan you'll find yourself getting overly excited and abandoning your exit strategy.

Your goal is to consistently make profits by coming up with a game plan and sticking to the strategy. Continuously changing your strategy in the middle of a position is a sure way to drain your account.

Education and Discipline

It is estimated that nearly 9 out of 10 new traders – or 90% - start off trading without a lack of knowledge, education or discipline. People are drawn to trading because they think it's a get-rich scheme and that if you're lucky, you'll win more than you will lose. This is called gambling, not trading and is a very dangerous misconception that will lead to consistent losses.

While there are hundreds of books and educational websites that can go deeper into this topic, to put this into the simplest of terms you have to understand what drives the markets including the different factors that can affect prices. When you enter a trade, you are not picking up stock certificates from a dusty shelf and then selling it back to that shelf. You are buying from another trader. If you're taking a bullish stance (price will go up), you are buying from someone with a bearish stance (price will go down). It's as simple as that.

When it comes to discipline, one of the most valuable trading tips I can share is to avoid *emotional* trading. This includes setting mental or physical stop-loss orders and taking profits when your trade reaches your predetermined price point versus impulsive trading based on some emotional reaction that has you going against your original plan. It means not chasing a stock after you sold for a profit because you are now second-guessing yourself and think it might go higher. It might. But it might not. And changing strategy mid-stream can result in giving back all of your profits and then some.

CHAPTER 4

TRAITS OF SUCCESSFUL TRADERS

Regardless of the type of trader you identify as, whether day trader, swing trader or longer term investor there are specific traits that separate the successful trader from the unsuccessful trader:

1. **A specific trading strategy**

   The trader has done their homework including analysis and price entry/exit points and knows exactly why they are getting into the trade. Once in the trade, they will stick with the plan. If it's intended to be a short-term swing trade they are not going to change mid-stream and suddenly become an investor if the stock moves goes against their original strategy.

2. **Emotional Intelligence & Discipline**

   Trading can be fun and rewarding but often times can be highly emotional and many traders find it challenging to stick with their original objective during market volatility. Fear, greed and hope can cause traders to make rash decisions, take on excessive risk and stay with losing positions. Sticking to a well thought out trading plan will improve your bottom line, reduce stress and keep you focused and on track.

3. **Resiliency**

   Great performances come from being able to bounce back quickly from a losing trade and moving on to the next potential winner.

4. **Trade With Risk Capital Only**

   Never trade with "scared" money. This is money that you cannot afford to lose such as emergency savings, kids' college fund or second mortgage. Your trading capital should never come from a source that would negatively alter you or your family's ability to continue your current lifestyle.

5. **Keeping a Trading Record**

   Keep a record of your trades so that you can easily look back to see what is working or not working. Looking at common denominators in good and not so good trades will help you determine your strengths and weaknesses.

6. **Find a Technique That Works and Stick With It**

   Most successful traders have only a few techniques that they consistently use to take money out of the markets. There are many, many trading strategies out there and what works for one may not work so well for another. Pick the one(s) that make the most sense to you and stick with it. Too many new traders get into the bad habit of constantly trying out a new trading strategy before they've become proficient in even one. This will have even the most resilient trader frustrated and ultimately worse off financially.

7. **Don't Change Strategies in the Middle of a Trade**

   Successful traders have the discipline to stick with their original game plan and do not change strategies in the middle of a trade. Simply put, if you are intending to be in a stock for 3 to 5 days for a bullish move but the stock moves quickly against you, don't change your strategy to a long-term investor. Your original analysis had you thinking the stock would have short, upward movement. Suddenly becoming a long-term investor means you are now trading based on hope as well as tying up your capital. This probably sounds like a regurgitation of #1, however, it's worth repeating.

Now that you have some idea of how to approach trading and investing, let me share with you the two types of analysis used by traders and investors – fundamental and technical analysis.

CHAPTER 5

FUNDAMENTAL AND TECHNICAL ANALYSIS EXPLAINED

There are two main types of analysis used by traders and investors to support their trading decisions – fundamental and technical analysis.

Fundamental Analysis: This type of analysis involves evaluating the intrinsic value of an asset by examining related economic, financial, and other qualitative and quantitative factors. Fundamental analysis looks at the underlying factors that could influence the asset's price, such as company financials (e.g., revenue, earnings, debt), industry trends, macroeconomic indicators and overall market conditions. Fundamental traders aim to identify assets that are undervalued or overvalued compared to their intrinsic worth. They believe that over time the market will correct any discrepancies between the asset's intrinsic value and its current market price.

Technical Analysis: Technical analysis involves studying historical market data, primarily price and volume, to forecast future price movements. Traders who use technical analysis believe that historical price patterns and trends can repeat and that by identifying these patterns, they can predict future price directions. Technical analysts use various tools and techniques, such as chart patterns, trend lines, moving averages, oscillators, and other indicators to analyze price data and make trading decisions. The focus is on identifying entry and exit points based on the chart patterns and signals generated by these tools.

While fundamental analysis deals with the underlying value of an asset, technical analysis focuses on historical price behavior. Traders may use either or both methods depending on their trading strategies and preferences. Some traders combine both types of analysis to gain a more comprehensive view of the markets to make well-informed trading decisions.

My preference for all of my trades is the use of technical analysis.

Most trading platforms offer a vast array of technical indicators needed for when charting out a particular stock. Examples include Moving Averages, Relative Strength Index (RSI), Moving Average Convergence Divergence (MACD), Bollinger Bands, Fibonacci Retracement, Algorithmic trading platforms, and Volume to name a few. Day traders in particular often rely on a combination of these technical indicators as well as live news feeds.

My strategy encompasses two simple indicators – Bollinger Bands and Volume.

CHAPTER 6
BOLLINGER BANDS

Developed in 1983 by John Bollinger, these trading bands are plotted at standard deviation levels above and below a moving average, such as the 20-day moving average. Because standard deviation measures volatility, the bands widen during volatile markets and contract during calmer periods. Bollinger Bands help show visually when a stock may be overbought or oversold. If the stock price breaks the upper band, it indicates an overbought situation. The reverse is if the price breaks the lower band; this would indicate an oversold situation.

A Bollinger Band consists of a middle band (moving average) as well as upper and lower bands and are typically plotted two standard deviations above and below a moving average. This means that about 95% of a security's historical price movement is likely contained within the two bands.

The idea behind Bollinger Bands is that the majority of price movements should occur within the range between the upper and lower bands. However, price movements outside of these bands can and do occur, especially during periods of high volatility or significant market events.

When a stock's price moves outside of the Bollinger Bands, it can indicate either an overbought or oversold condition, potentially signaling a reversal or a continuation of the trend, depending on the context and other technical indicators. Traders and analysts often pay attention to such occurrences as they may provide insights into potential price movements.

CHAPTER 7

VOLUME - YES, IT MATTERS

Volume is an important concept in technical analysis, and it refers to the number of shares or other financial instrument traded during a given period. In the context of trading, volume is used to gain insights into the strength and significance of price movements, confirm trends and identify potential reversals. Here are some ways volume is used in technical analysis for trading:

1. **Confirmation of Price Movements:** Volume can confirm the validity of price movements. For example, when a stock price rises, an increase in trading volume suggests that the price movement is supported by a large number of buyers, making it more reliable. Conversely, if the price rises, but the volume is low, it may indicate weak interest from market participants, and the price movement may be less reliable.

2. **Trend Analysis:** Analyzing volume alongside price trends helps identify the strength of a trend. In an uptrend, higher trading volumes during upward price movements indicate strong buying interest, reinforcing the bullish trend. Similarly, in a downtrend, higher volumes during downward price movements indicate strong selling pressure, confirming the bearish trend.

3. **Reversal Signals:** Volume can also help identify potential trend reversals. A significant increase in volume following a prolonged uptrend or downtrend may signal a trend reversal. For example, a sudden surge in volume during a downtrend could indicate that selling pressure is reaching exhaustion, and a potential reversal to an uptrend might be imminent.

4. **Support and Resistance Levels:** Volume can be used to validate support and resistance levels. When a price approaches a support level and the volume increases, it suggests a stronger level of demand at that price, making the support level more significant. Conversely, when a price approaches a resistance level and the volume increases, it indicates higher selling interest and reinforces the importance of the resistance level.

5. **Divergence Analysis:** Volume divergence occurs when the price is moving in one direction, but the trading volume is moving in the opposite direction. This can be a sign of a potential trend reversal. For example, during an uptrend,

if the price continues to make higher highs, but the volume decreases or remains flat, it may indicate that the trend is losing momentum and could reverse.

6. **Breakout Confirmation:** Traders often use volume to confirm breakouts from chart patterns or key technical levels. A breakout accompanied by high volume suggests a strong conviction among traders, increasing the likelihood of a sustained price movement in the direction of the breakout.

An important component of volume is the "average shares traded", also known as the average daily trading volume. This is an essential metric to consider when evaluating a stock for potential investment. The average daily trading volume represents the number of shares traded on average each day over a specific period, such as the past three months or six months. It helps gauge the liquidity and activity of a stock in the market.

In particular, it is important that the stocks you are trading have sufficient liquidity. For many day traders, the minimum requirement is a daily average of around 1 million. Day traders need to implement their entry and exit strategies quickly and with ease. For swing/short term traders, the volume requirement may be closer to 300,000 to 500,000.

My strategies fall into the latter and for the most part, I like to stick with stocks that have a daily average of closer to 500,000 and higher.

Now that we've covered Bollinger Bands and Volume we need a helpful charting tool to plot these two indicators. Among the various chart styles – bar charts, mountain charts, etc. - my preferred chart style is Candlestick.

CHAPTER 8
CANDLESTICK CHARTING SIMPLIFIED

Candlestick charting is among the most popular tool used by most professional traders. Candlestick charts have a "real body" that represents the price range between the open and close of that day's trading. If the real body is filled it means the close was lower than the open. If the real body is clear it means the close was higher than the open. If the price range exceeded the open and or close on either end, the candlestick will have a wick to reflect this.

Candlesticks reflect investor sentiment on stock or other security prices and are used to help determine when to enter and exit trades.

Let's look at an example of Hershey (HSY) on a candlestick chart using the two technical indicators – Bollinger Bands and Volume – for a 5-month period.

Without any real experience reading candlestick charts one could probably analyze fairly quickly that during the periods of late January through early May, HSY was in a clear uptrend. The stock then stalled in a tight pricing range until mid-May when the stock reversed into a downtrend.

The Bollinger Bands (using a 20-day moving average) helps the trader see potential overbought and oversold conditions, such as in late April when the stock consistently moved above or near the upper band, potentially indicating the stock may be overbought.

Let's take a smaller time frame of this chart between 3/10/23 and 5/19/23.

On 4/26 (orange arrow), the stock opened at 262.98 with a high of 263.36, a low of 260.98 and end-of-day close at 261.75. Hence, the candlestick is solid since it closed lower than the open (a bearish day).

The next business day on 4/27 (green arrow), the stock opened at 264.27, had a range of 263.71 to 273.42 and then closed end-of-day at 273.33. Because the stock closed higher than the open, the candlestick is clear (bullish day).

Important to note is the volume on 4/27 was around 1.8M, which was a much higher than the stock's average trading day of closer to 985k. When a stock experiences higher-than-normal trading volume and its price moves in a certain direction (up or down), this can suggest that the price movement has a stronger backing from market participants. Higher volume confirms the strength of the price movement.

Let's look at another chart - GameStop.

GameStop is a stock that became a popular meme stock in early January 2021. You will quickly note the difference in price volatility as compared to Hershey.

Looking at a 4-month chart, on 3/22/23 the stock had a significant gap up on the open at 26.60 with a day's range of 23.05 thru 27.00 and an end-of-day close at 23.87. The wicks on either end show the price range (high and low) and since the stock closed below the open the candlestick is solid.

Note that this stock closed as 17.65 the prior trading day and then gapped up the next trading day at the open at 26.60, a difference of almost 9.00!

For the record, this is not a stock I would consider for my strategic slide strategy nor long-term investment. Simply put, meme stocks are stocks that experience significant price volatility and trading activity driven primarily by online communities and social media platforms and internet memes rather than traditional fundamental or technical factors. You might win big one day, but then give it all up the next day when convinced it's "going to the moon."

Now that I've shared my two favorite indicators – Bollinger Bands and Volume – as well as a beginner's basic on candle stick charting, I'm excited to now share how I approach one my favorite trading strategies.

CHAPTER 9

BREAKING DOWN THE STRATEGY

To recap, the strategic slide strategy incorporates a concept of averaging down which involves gradually increasing your position in a security by buying more shares or units as the price decreases. Here's how averaging down works:

- Initial Purchase: An investor buys a certain amount of an asset at a specific price.
- Price Decline: After the initial purchase, if the price of the asset decreases, the investor may perceive it as an opportunity to buy more of the asset at a lower price.
- Additional Purchases: The investor buys more of the asset at the lower price, thereby reducing the average price at which they own the asset. This means that the investor needs the asset's price to rise less in order to break even or make a profit.

The idea behind averaging down is that the investor believes in the long-term potential of the asset and considers the price drop to be a temporary setback. By buying more at a lower price, they can potentially benefit from a larger price increase in the future.

There are many different ways to approach this strategy. Some investors may look for companies with good fundamentals yet the stock is experiencing a possible temporary setback due to current economic landscape, thus buying the dips with the assumption the stock will eventually recover. These investors have a longer-term view and are willing to wait out the short-term volatility.

Other traders may be monitoring a stock that is in a clear uptrend and buy on price dips multiple times while later selling at new highs and new resistance levels.

The way I approach this strategy is a little different. I look for stocks with two criteria points:

- Has formed a strong, consolidated base over a period of time
- Is trading closer to the stock's 52-week low

When I refer to a base, I am talking about when a stock consolidates in a base pattern. This is often referred to as "building a base" or "forming a base." Base formation is a common technical analysis term used by traders and investors to describe a period of price consolidation and relative stability in a stock's price.

During this phase, the stock's price tends to trade within a defined range and there is no clear trend in either direction, up or down. The base formation is typically characterized by a series of higher lows and lower highs, indicating that buyers and sellers are roughly in balance.

Let's look at an example.

Below is a four-month time period of International Paper (IP).

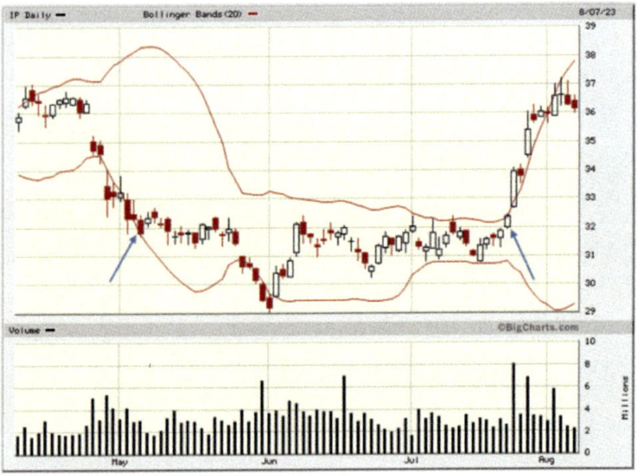

After falling from previous highs, IP formed a base beginning on May 4, 2023. The stock continued to form and trade in a consolidated base through July 24 until the stock gapped upwards the following trading day – July 25 - and continued an upward trading pattern towards previous highs.

See blue arrows indicating consolidation range between 5/4 and 7/24.

The concept of base building is crucial in technical analysis as it can signal potential future price movements. Once the base is formed, traders often look for breakouts or breakdowns from the base pattern. A breakout occurs when the stock's price rises above the upper boundary of the base, suggesting a potential upward trend while a breakdown happens when the stock's price falls below the lower boundary, indicating a potential downward trend.

While you can trade within a base at any price levels, be it in a higher or lower historical price range, for this particular strategy the criteria is it must be in the lower historical price range and closer to its 52-week low price.

Here's my methodology and rationale behind this strategy.

The 52-week low provides insights into the price range within which a stock has been trading over the past year. When a stock's price is close to or at its 52-week low, it may be an indication that the stock is currently trading at a relatively low valuation compared to its recent history. This may attract value investors who see the stock as potentially undervalued and a buying opportunity.

For me, it's an additional supporting indicator and level of confidence that the stock is not going to suddenly do a free-fall as can happen if the stock is basing in a price range that is, say, 50% up from its 52-week low. In other words, I don't want to catch a falling knife. You can certainly find profitable opportunities in stocks that are basing in their upper price range but that will require keeping a closer eye for sudden dramatic drops, a.k.a., oversold conditions in which you must be prepared to exit quickly while accepting you may take a loss.

Therefore, my goal is to find a stock that has been in a steady base and to watch for an entry point near the low price of this base as well as not being too far off from its 52-week low price. As the price begins to come close to the lower end of this base I will take a position with the anticipation that it may have further downward movement, thus leading me to buy additional shares – hence, a strategic slide.

For example, if XYZ has been trading between 8 and 11 and its 52-week low is 6.80, I am looking for an entry point close to 8 with the understanding that the stock could go break through 8, heading towards its next support level of 6.80. And if that happens, I will buy additional shares.

Keep in mind, I'm only doing this with strong stocks of well-established companies in which I have high confidence that the stock will bounce back up sooner than later. I wouldn't use this strategy in stocks that have no meaningful historical pricing and proof of longevity, such as a company with a recent Initial Public Offering (IPO).

As far as my exit strategy, though I'm banking on the stock to come near or even a bit below the 52-week low I'm realistic enough to know that I cannot pick tops and bottoms. If I don't have a significant position in the stock and the stock dips a bit below the 52-week low I will give it time to reverse. However, if it begins to sink further and further I will want to limit my losses. For me, that might be 5-10% below the 52-week low. A significant drop could indicate a material change in the company's fundamentals that I'm not aware of or change in market conditions, such as a recession. The goal is to have more wins than losses – and sticking to the trading plan should ensure just that.

Now, let's look at the Strategic Slide strategy in action.

CHAPTER 10

THE STRATEGIC SLIDE IN ACTION

Upon finding an ideal stock that has formed a strong base I have found that not only can you have a high rate of success in making a profit, it is actually possible to achieve multiple profitable trades by entering and exiting the stock during its basing period.

I did just that with Ford (F) - a long established company stock.

Between 2/23/23 and 5/26/23 I played this strategy six times and profited every single time – not one loss. And in only one case did I not average down as the stock took a move upwards.

My total profit for this twelve-week period was $20,500.35. That's an average of about $1,708 per week! Here are my results:

DATE	TRANSACTION ID	DESCRIPTION	QUANTITY	SYMBOL	PRICE	AMOUNT
2/23/2023	48334630951	Bought 5000 F @ 12.3299	5000	F	12.3299	$ (61,649.50)
2/27/2023	48386030171	Bought 5000 F @ 12.0099	5000	F	12.0099	$ (60,049.50)
3/6/2023	48562705096	Sold 10000 F @ 12.9507	10000	F	12.9507	$129,504.51
						$ 7,805.51
3/13/2023	48702801734	Bought 5000 F @ 11.7697	5000	F	11.7697	$ (58,848.50)
3/15/2023	48757269610	Bought 5000 F @ 11.3699	5000	F	11.3699	$ (56,849.50)
3/17/2023	48818279164	Bought 5000 F @ 11.2199	5000	F	11.2199	$ (56,099.50)
3/22/2023	48890368269	Sold 15000 F @ 11.7104	15000	F	11.7104	$175,652.41
						$ 3,854.91
3/24/2023	48958615328	Bought 5000 F @ 11.2699	5000	F	11.2699	$ (56,349.50)
3/29/2023	49054598914	Sold 5000 F @ 11.8601	5000	F	11.8601	$ 59,299.30
						$ 2,949.80
4/19/2023	49524635550	Bought 4000 F @ 12.215	4000	F	12.215	$ (48,860.00)
4/20/2023	49544834037	Bought 4000 F @ 11.7183	4000	F	11.7183	$ (46,873.20)
4/26/2023	49654296902	Bought 4000 F @ 11.58	4000	F	11.58	$ (46,320.00)
5/8/2023	49929884118	Sold 12000 F @ 12.01	12000	F	12.01	$144,117.11
						$ 2,063.91
5/10/2023	49981125367	Bought 3000 F @ 11.78	3000	F	11.78	$ (35,340.00)
5/12/2023	50025186082	Bought 3000 F @ 11.665	3000	F	11.665	$ (34,995.00)
5/16/2023	50072991712	Bought 3000 F @ 11.4857	3000	F	11.4857	$ (34,457.10)
5/23/2023	50199460575	Sold 9000 F @ 11.8507	9000	F	11.8507	$106,654.14
						$ 1,862.04
5/24/2023	50220972103	Bought 3000 F @ 11.415	3000	F	11.415	$ (34,245.00)
5/24/2023	50224265846	Bought 3000 F @ 11.25	3000	F	11.25	$ (33,750.00)
5/26/2023	50269613429	Sold 6000 F @ 11.6601	6000	F	11.6601	$ 69,959.17
						$ 1,964.17
Net Total:						$ 20,500.35

Why Ford?

Ford fit my criteria. It is a strong, long established company/stock, exceeded my average volume requirement and the consolidated basing period was trading closer to its 52-week low.

I initially came across Ford in mid-January 2023 when a buddy of mine mentioned he was finally gaining back some of his losses (he's more of a longer-term buy and hold kind of investor). After pulling a few historical charts and recognizing the predictable ranges, I began monitoring Ford in earnest.

Here is a chart taken between 5/1/22 through 1/13/23, right around when I began monitoring the stock. Note that Ford reflects a continual basing pattern with no strong desire to make a major break out of its current support and resistance levels. In other words, no continued climb nor decline.

What also caught my attention is that this stock did not appear to be a particularly volatile stock. In fact, some may consider this stock's trading pattern to be a bit boring unlike a stock such as GameStop that will have you hanging onto the edge of your seat.

For me, boring adds another element of reduced risks.

Here is my thought process for how I approached monitoring and coming up with a first entry point.

In early February 2023, the stock hit a high of 14.60 and then slowly began making its way back down. Referencing the chart's timeframe (5/1/22 through 1/13/23), I noted its previous lowest price points had been hovering above 10.39 (early July 2022) and 10.90 (late December) with the 52-week low being 10.39. I decided a price in the low 12.00 range would be appropriate for an initial purchase and then average down from there.

As far as a potential exit price, since the recent areas of resistance had been closer from 12.90 to 13.90 I'm looking at somewhere above 12.80. You don't have to implement complicated math, it's really just looking at prior support and resistance levels when it comes to buying and selling, knowing you'll never call tops and bottoms consistently.

On 2/23, I see my opportunity and buy 5000 shares @12.32. On 2/24, the stock hits a low of 11.75 with a day's range of 11.75 – 11.97 but at this point I do nothing as I'm waiting to see if it goes down further.

On 2/27, the stock bounces up a bit with the low of the day being higher than the previous day's low and I am now thinking it may be poised for a reversal. Therefore, I buy 5000 additional shares @12, which still has me averaging down from my original purchase price. My per-share price is now roughly 12.16.

The stock continues to climb and after a little over a week and a half, on 3/6 the stock hits a trading range of 12.93 – 13.18. Since this is above the lower end right within the range I was looking to be in,

I move forward and sell all 10,000 shares at 12.95, netting me a total profit of $7,805.

Here are my trades 2/23/23 through 3/6 (orange arrow indicates BUY; green indicates SELL):

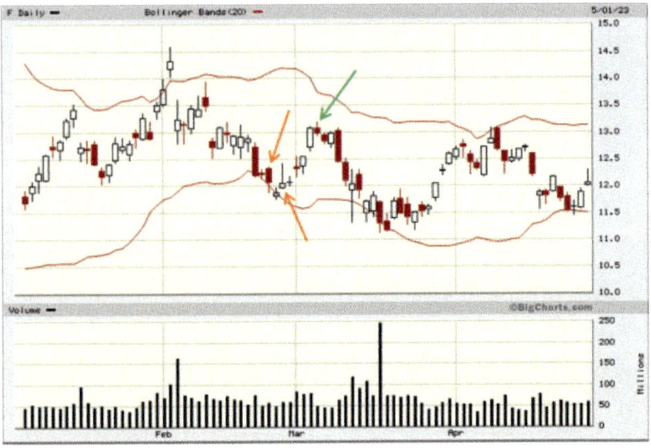

Not bad for a week and half's worth of efforts.

Now let me stop right here for a moment so that I can explain the emotional effect of making that initial first purchase.

When an investor purchases stock with the intent that the stock is poised to rise, it's an immediate emotional roller coaster ride. There is continuous checking in to see if the stock is moving upward as planned. If the stock is in fact drifting lower, panic and second-guessing often starts to set in. This type of trading strategy often has investors, particularly novices new to the game, exiting too quickly and taking a loss mainly because he or she was only banking on the stock to go up with zero to little wiggle room for perhaps a bit more pullback.

The strangely wonderful thing about this particular lower-risk averaging down strategy is that I am at complete peace with the stock going down further as my plan already encompassed adding additional shares (averaging down). However, if the stock reverses and heads back up, I'm just going to make an earlier profit.

I think the emotional aspect is important to note because at the end of the day, we get into trades to make money, period. And for someone who has traded various styles and patterns over the past 25 years, I will say this is one of the least stressful styles of trading for me.

Now that Ford has shown me proof of results as well as the potential for further profitable results, I continue to monitor for the next lows and go on to successfully buy and sell shares multiple times. Let's discuss my 3/13 through 3/29 trades.

After my previous sell on 3/6, the stock begins to move back down towards the lower end of the base range. On 3/13, I buy 5000 shares @11.76. On 3/14, the stock bounces up a bit so I sit tight as it may reverse (remember, if it goes up I'm still making money). On 3/15, the stock gaps down and I buy an additional 5000 shares @11.36. Then on 3/17, I make an additional purchase of 5000 shares @11.21.

At this point, the stock is trading below its recent lows but still above the 52-week low of 10.90. The stock tests this support level the following day and then on 3/21 appears to make its journey back upwards. However, on 3/22 I sense the stock is struggling (just looking at the candlestick of the day) and decide to sell all 15000 shares @11.71, netting me a total profit of $3,854.

Here are my trades 2/23/23 through 3/22:

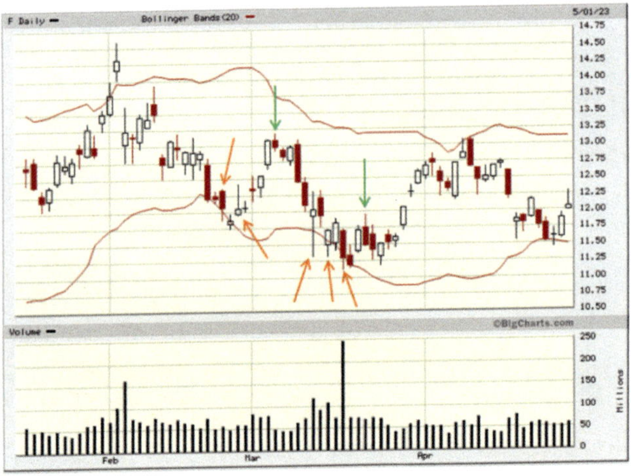

Let's go over my next trade for the timeframe between 3/24 and 3/29.

After my previous sell off on 3/22, the stock begins to drift lower and on 3/24 I decide to make an initial purchase of 5000 shares @11.26. The stock reverses upward the next trading day and so I hang on to see where this takes me.

At this point, I have two sell prices in mind – somewhere near 11.90 based on the recent resistance levels (3/16 through 3/22) or if the stock appears to be particularly strong, I'm looking at the resistance levels closer to 13 based on 3/3 through 3/9 activity.

On 3/29, the stock gaps up and at some point hits a high of 12.06. I'm not sure if there's going to be continued strength and because it surpassed my 11.90 sell point I go ahead and decide to sell at 11.86, netting me a profit of $2,950.

Here are my trades 2/23/23 through 3/29:

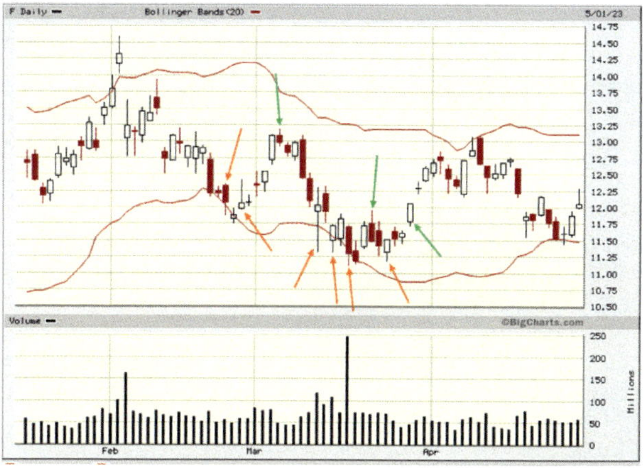

The stock continued on an upward climb and on 4/12/23, Ford hit a high of 13.08 and then reversed its journey down. On 4/19, the stock has a strong move down and I decide to re-enter with a purchase of 4000 shares @12.21 (day's range was 12.17 – 12.60).

The stock takes another dip the following trading day and on 4/20, I purchase an additional 4000 shares @11.71. At this point, I'm looking at the more recent support levels of 11.15 – 11.18 as my rational for continuing to average down.

After a few days of basing, I purchase an additional 4000 shares @11.58. At this point, it appears the stock is in a new basing period with support levels at just below 11.50 and resistance levels just above 12.00. I watch the stock test this a few times and then decide to sell all 12000 shares @12.01, netting me a profit of $2,063.91.

Here are my trades 4/19/23 through 5/8:

Let's now go over my last set of trades, 5/10/23 through 5/26.

On 5/10, I buy 3000 shares @ 11.78. My thought process was this price was close to previous price levels of resistance based on the previous highs within this base. Additionally, the day's direction of the stock looked poised to close below the open of the day. Therefore, I'm anticipating the stock to go lower and happily grab additional shares. However, if it happens to go higher then that's okay too - I'm still making money.

On 5/12, the stock is slowly declining and I buy another 3000 shares @11.66.The stock continues to dip and on 5/16, I buy another 3000 shares @11.48.

At this point, I'm comfortable sticking with my position of 9,000 shares as the low within this base is 11.44 and with a 52-week low of 10.90, I'm feeling pretty confident that an upward move is imminent.

Ford continues to slowly climb over the next several days. On May 23, the stock reaches a high of 11.91 and after watching it come back down a bit I decide to take a profit and sell all 9,000 shares @11.85. This nets me a total profit of $1,862.

On the very next trading day, the stock takes a strong dip due to overall market weakness as well as possibly reacting to a recall.

Often times, bad news brings with it buying opportunities. However, you have to be careful and determine just how bad the news really is. Reactions to market conditions such as the above are pretty normal and typically short-lived whereas an announcement such as a company is filing for bankruptcy will likely impact the stock negatively for a long time.

I decide that the news is not too severe and on 5/24 buy 3,000 shares @11.41. Later in the day, the stock dips lower and I buy an additional 3,000 shares @11.25, which just happens to be the low of the trading day. I decide to stay put with 6,000 shares as I'm right off the support levels of this base.

On May 26, the stock springs upwards and as it's blown through its previous resistance, I decide to sell all 6,000 shares @11.66 giving me a net profit of $1,964.

Hurray, right?

Well, guess what happened the next business trading day?

On Tuesday, May 30 the stock gaps up on the open at 12.65 with a tight range of 12.51-12.78 and a close of 12.59. The suggested reasoning behind this strong movement was due to Ford Motor Company being upgraded by Jefferies Group LLC, an independent investment bank and financial services company that is headquartered in New York City.

Note blue arrow in following chart:

Where is that crystal ball when you need one?

So, what do you think I did? Jump in and hang on for the ride? Stay put and keep my hands in my pocket? I stayed put, and here's why.

A stock that has surged quickly, particularly on news-driven data can lead to overvaluation, thus causing the stock to tumble right back to where it was or lower. Chasing stocks is allowing one's emotions to take over, perhaps fear of missing out. Such impulsive actions are not aligned with a well thought-out investment strategy and emotional trading will surely cause a trader losses over time.

Here are my trades 4/19/2023 through 5/26:

Let me tell you what would have happened if I had panicked-purchased and held on through the close. The next day the stock tanked and would have dropped through my re-entry, previous day's purchase price. That would have completely shaken me out of the stock, giving back previous gains. It should be noted that the stock dropped down the next day as well, but then slowly began climbing back up. So then I would have been even more ticked to note that I panic-sold and lost previous gains that I didn't need to.

This is why it's important to stick to a particular strategy. At the end of the day, I am happy because I still made money.

So there you have it – my six trades in one stock over a 12-week period using the refined approach of the strategic slide strategy.

CHAPTER 11

ACHIEVING SUCCESS WITH A BEGINNER'S PORTFOLIO

Now, let me point out that you will have no doubt noticed that my trades involved taking reasonably large positions representing capital that perhaps you don't quite yet have at your disposal or you simply don't want to put your money where your experience level isn't quite at yet.

The good news is, you absolutely can implement this strategy with a much more modest portfolio to begin with. In fact, I highly recommend you start out slowly in the beginning by purchasing smaller positions and allow yourself the time to gain experience and confidence before ramping up to larger positions. It's always a good idea to keep your exposure risk to a minimum as you would with any new strategy you are looking to learn.

To help give you a visual perspective, I have revised my original trades into smaller positions so that you can see what the trades and results of a modest portfolio of less than $10,000 would have resulted in:

DATE	TRANSACTION ID	DESCRIPTION	QUANTITY	SYMBOL	PRICE	COMMISSION	AMOUNT
2/23/2023	48334630951	Bought 5000 F @ 12.3299	250	F	12.3299	0	-3082.475
2/27/2023	48386030171	Bought 5000 F @ 12.0099	250	F	12.0099	0	-3002.475
3/6/2023	48562705096	Sold 10000 F @ 12.9507	500	F	12.9507	0	6475.35
							390.4
3/13/2023	48702801734	Bought 5000 F @ 11.7697	250	F	11.7697	0	-2942.425
3/15/2023	48757269610	Bought 5000 F @ 11.3699	250	F	11.3699	0	-2842.475
3/17/2023	48818279164	Bought 5000 F @ 11.2199	250	F	11.2199	0	-2804.975
3/22/2023	48890368269	Sold 15000 F @ 11.7104	750	F	11.7104	0	8782.8
							192.925
3/24/2023	48958615328	Bought 5000 F @ 11.2699	250	F	11.2699	0	-2817.475
3/29/2023	49054598914	Sold 5000 F @ 11.8601	250	F	11.8601	0	2965.025
							147.55
3/31/2023	49135061771	Bought 4000 F @ 12.4499	250	F	12.4499	0	-3110
4/10/2023	49352973543	Sold 4000 F @ 12.6704	4000	F	12.6704	0	3167.6
							57.6
4/19/2023	49524635550	Bought 4000 F @ 12.215	250	F	12.215	0	-3053.75
4/20/2023	49544834037	Bought 4000 F @ 11.7183	250	F	11.7183	0	-2929.575
4/26/2023	49654296902	Bought 4000 F @ 11.58	250	F	11.58	0	-2895
5/8/2023	49929884118	Sold 12000 F @ 12.01	750	F	12.01	0	9007.5
							129.175
5/10/2023	49981125367	Bought 3000 F @ 11.78	250	F	11.78	0	-2945
5/12/2023	50025186082	Bought 3000 F @ 11.665	250	F	11.665	0	-2916.25
5/16/2023	50072991712	Bought 3000 F @ 11.4857	250	F	11.4857	0	-2871.425
5/23/2023	50199460575	Sold 9000 F @ 11.8507	750	F	11.8507	0	8888.025
							155.35
5/24/2023	50220972103	Bought 3000 F @ 11.415	250	F	11.415	0	-2853.75
5/24/2023	50224265846	Bought 3000 F @ 11.25	250	F	11.25	0	-2812.5
5/26/2023	50269613429	Sold 6000 F @ 11.6601	500	F	11.6601	0	5830
							163.75
							$1,236.75

While $1,236 may not seem as impressive as $20,500, it should be considered a good start to your trading and investing future.

Keep in mind that trading profitably requires a combination of skill, experience, and emotional discipline as well as time and patience to navigate the complexities of the market, make informed decisions and ride out inevitable fluctuations. The purpose of this book was to help both the novice and seasoned trader discover a lower risk and reliable trading strategy that can be used over and over resulting in consistent profits.

This concludes the nuts and bolts of my Strategic Slide strategy.

CONCLUSION

I really hope that you come out of this excited in having found an innovative, new approach that not only seeks to enhance profitability but also aims to mitigate risk, providing a robust framework for capital preservation in every type of market condition. I truly believe anyone can find long-term success in the stock market.

Remember, consistency and patience are the cornerstones of successful trading. By adhering to these principles, you'll be well-quipped to navigate the dynamic world of stock trading and achieve your financial goals, one "slide" at a time!

Pamela S Batoon

ABOUT THE AUTHOR

Pamela Batoon has been an independent trader and investor in the financial markets for over twenty-five years. During this time, she has experienced both the highs and lows of market volatility and has approached all styles of trading including day and swing trading, all while continuing to dive into as much training and material on the intricacies and "secrets" of the markets as possible. Over time, she has come to the conclusion that there really are no complicated secrets and that all anyone really needs are a few tools and simple concepts to make consistent profits in any market conditions.

Made in the USA
Las Vegas, NV
09 July 2025

24659938R00033